Through the Year in

CHINA

Frances Wood

Batsford Academic and Educational Ltd London

Acknowledgments
The Author and Publishers thank the following for their kind permission to use the copyright illustrations in this book: Anglo-Chinese Educational Institute for the photographs on pages 14 (bottom), 26 (left) and 32-33; Camera Press Ltd for the photographs on pages 13, 16, 21, 30 (top), 34, 35, 37, 41 (bottom), 53, 55, 58, 65; Richard and Sally Greenhill for the photographs on pages 8, 9, 10, 11, 12, 14 (top), 15, 18, 20, 23, 25, 26 (right), 27, 30 (bottom), 32, 36, 38, 40 (left), 41 (top), 42, 43, 44, 47, 48, 49, 51, 52, 59, 60, 61, 62, 64, 67, 68; John Massey Stewart for the photographs on pages 24, 40 (right). The maps were drawn by Mr R. Britto. The pictures were researched by Pat Hodgson.

Typeset by Tek-art Ltd, London SE 20
and printed in Great Britain by
R.J. Acford Ltd
Chichester, Sussex
for the publishers
Batsford Academic and Educational Ltd,
an imprint of B T Batsford Ltd,
4 Fitzhardinge Street
London W1H 0AH

ISBN 0 7134 3968 8

Contents

Introduction

China may seem different from Britain and the west in every way.

There are differences in the calendar. In traditional China the New Year began some time in February, not on 1 January, for the Chinese used to use the lunar calendar which is less rigid than ours, and all their festivals were therefore relatively movable feasts, like our Easter.

In China today daily life encompasses both the traditions of the past and the new systems of a socialist state. And so, during the year, both lunar festivals and events like workers' holidays and National Day are celebrated.

One of the most "different" things about China is the language, which has developed in a unique way into a complicated system of characters, with no alphabet. This makes it very difficult to transliterate (express) Chinese words into the roman alphabet. Until January 1979 most English-language books on China used the form of spelling of the Wade-Giles system of transcription, while the Germans and French had their own systems. Then in January 1979 the Chinese began to use their own system of writing Chinese words in the roman alphabet — called *pinyin* — and most western publications now use this form.

For the ordinary reader this has meant getting used to a new way of spelling. Mao Tse-tung (Wade-Giles system) is now written Mao Zedong (pinyin), Chou En-lai has become Zhou Enlai; Teng Hsiao-p'ing has become Deng Xiaoping, Peking is Beijing; Canton is Guangzhou, etc.

In this book we have used the pinyin system of spelling, with the old Wade-Giles version of the word in brackets the first time it appears. Pinyin is in fact a more accurate system than the Wade-Giles one as well as being more internationally accepted.

As we follow through the year in China, you will see that it is basically the same sequence of seasons, of school terms, of seasonal foods and fruits as it is for us. But it is the many different details within that sequence which makes China interesting.

China ▷

4

January

The Chinese Calendar

The western calendar has been used in China since 1911, though it was not fully adopted until 1949.

In 1911, when the last imperial dynasty of the Qing was overthrown, the new government decided to drop the traditional lunar calendar and named 1 January 1911 "January 1st of the 1st year of the Republic". But while the days of the western calendar were followed, the years were still numbered in the old way, like the years in a dynasty or reign. In the past, whenever a new dynasty had been founded, it had been given a new and auspicious name (the Ming dynasty meant the "bright" dynasty, the Qing was the "clear" or "pure" dynasty). Each new Emperor within the dynasty was also given a

"reign name", and the years were counted from one, within each reign. So, for example, 1746 was called "the 10th year of the Qianlong reign of the Qing dynasty" (the Qianlong Emperor ruled from 1736-1795), and 1627 was called "the 5th year of the reign of the Kangxi Emperor", and so on. The new government in 1911 continued this system, calling that year "the 1st year of the Republic".

The Republic of China (on the island of Taiwan) still counts the years this way, calling 1981, for example, "the 70th year of the Republic". But the government of the People's Republic of China (which rules all of China except Taiwan) broke with the traditional system in 1949. Since then the years have been described by number, just as in the west.

The Chinese calendar had far more complications than a series of reign names. Traditionally, it was a lunar calendar, following only the phases of the moon, and calendars printed today still show the dates in the lunar calendar, underneath the western-style dates. So, while 1 January is recognized as New

---

THE ANIMALS OF THE ZODIAC

Yet another way of marking the years in traditional China was according to the twelve-year cycle, represented by a series of twelve animals. These animals were also used to name the "hours" in a day (which were two hours long in old China). The astrological sign under which a person was born and the animal of their birth year were some of the points considered by fortune-tellers who were always consulted over important decisions, especially marriage. In simple terms, it was not a good idea for a man born in the year of the rat to marry a lady born in the year of the tiger or the snake, but astrologers could usually find other points that would reduce the danger if the couple really wanted to get married.

11 pm—1 am	Rat	1948
1—3 am	Ox	1949
3—5 am	Tiger	1950
5—7 am	Hare	1951
7—9 am	Dragon	1952
9—11 am	Snake	1953
11 am—1 pm	Horse	1954
1—3 pm	Goat	1955
3—5 pm	Monkey	1956
5—7 pm	Cock	1957
7—9 pm	Dog	1958
9—11 pm	Pig	1959 and so on.

Year's Day, it is not a holiday, for the celebrations come with the beginning of the lunar year which may fall in either January or February.

The lunar New Year (like our Easter) is movable, because the lunar year, following natural lunar months, comes to a total of only 354 days per year. The solar calendar is more precise but, even so, requires an extra day every leap year; the Chinese lunar calendar required a whole "intercalary month" seven times every nineteen years to keep even with the solar year.

As well as the lunar calendar, there was also an agricultural calendar which divided the year into twenty-four sections, according to the weather (you can find these divisions at the head of each month in the book). In China today, 1 January is recognized as a beginning, but it comes about a month before the lunar new year holiday and, for the peasant, who sees the year in agricultural terms, January begins with "slight cold" and ends with "great cold".

Some city workers have a day off on 1 January and for peasants in the north, January is a slack season. The ground is frozen so hard from November to March that no digging or planting or growth is possible and the peasants turn to secondary tasks like repair and maintenance of machinery and piling manure onto the fields to be dug in when the frosts end.

Beijing

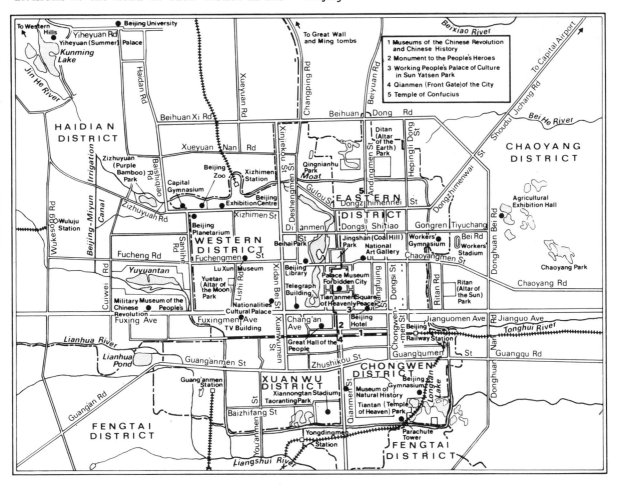

The Capital City, Beijing (Peking)

Though Beijing is the centre of government and an industrial city, it is also concerned with agriculture. The city has a population of about 8 million and spreads over 24,600 square kilometres, most of which is farmland supplying the city with food. On the outskirts of the city proper, towards the Summer Palace, university and college buildings stand in the middle of cultivated fields. And in the southwest, near the Marco Polo Bridge (a fine stone bridge built in 1192, with 140 tiny lions carved on the parapet), some of Beijing's largest factories like the February 7th Railway Engine Factory (named after a famous strike on the railways in 1923) are also surrounded by fields. Administratively, Beijing resembles other Chinese cities in its mixing of industry and agriculture.

Old Beijing, laid out in the Ming dynasty (1368-1644), was a walled city, covering a smaller area than today's vast municipality,

A group of visitors outside the Imperial Palace, Beijing.

and within the walls, it was a perfect example of traditional town planning. The Chinese believed that the north was the source of evil, and so buildings (and cities) faced south. In the centre of a grid of streets all running either north to south or east to west with absolute regularity, was the palace. The central status of the palace, both geographically and administratively, is emphasized by its colours. Amid the single-storeyed grey-roofed houses of the ordinary citizens, the Emperor's many-storeyed palace stood surrounded by high red walls and with all the roofs covered in bright yellow tiles, for yellow was the imperial colour.

Most of the important buildings of the past still stand in Beijing, though, sadly, the city walls were knocked down in the 1950s because their narrow double gates were slowing traffic. Modern buildings put up since 1949 include the Great Hall of the People, a national assembly hall that can seat 10,000, and the History Museum, both built in ten months in 1958. Despite much new building (especially of flats that increasingly replace the little low courtyard houses), the grid system of the streets remains unchanged. It is so regular that if you ask the way in Beijing, people use compass points rather than "left" and "right", saying: "If you go north along the street, you will find the shoe-mender on the west side of the road."

Beijing is divided into twelve districts, which are in turn sub-divided into smaller administrative units. The lowest level of local government is the neighbourhood committee which looks after the welfare of up to 15,000 families, providing schools, public security and basic welfare services. There are subsidiary, voluntary organizations like lane committees or even court-yard committees, staffed by volunteers (mostly housewives and retired people) who try to ensure that everyone within their area is well cared for. They see that the streets are clean, and old people looked after, that elementary public hygiene is taught — in schools, by public notices, in classes for housewives — and that the instructions are observed. These small committees and the involvement of local people in the management of their surroundings seem to break Beijing up into a series of villages where everyone knows everyone else. This has the effect of reducing crime, such as theft. As everybody's income and possessions are known by neighbours, it is difficult to suddenly acquire new possessions without enquiry. It also reduces marital problems because these are brought quickly into the open. Minor offences and marital disputes are usually handled by local people, often Communist Party Members, rather than by the courts.

The Communist Party

The role of the Communist Party in local affairs is strong. The Party sets out guide-line decisions on practically all aspects of life, and it is the duty of the 35 million Party members to see that these guide-lines

A typically straight street in Beijing. The low courtyard houses are entered through gates in the wall, like those on the right. The woman on the right has bought some vegetables for the evening meal.

Flats are replacing the single-storey courtyard houses, but the community feeling remains, because of the system of neighbourhood committees. These flats are in Shanghai, the most densely populated and most fashionable city in China (see page 58).

are reflected in local government, factory management and everywhere in society. Though the membership sounds huge, it represents only 4 per cent of the Chinese population and the "leading role" of the Party is the result of much discussion among members. The Party has organizations which parallel central and local government and the administrative committees of every commune, factory or school. Membership of Party Committee and administrative committee is quite likely to overlap, as Party members tend (although this is not always the case) to be respected members of society, thus able to mediate in local affairs that do not call for court intervention.

Looking into the courtyard of an old-style Chinese house.

February

"Beginning of spring; rain water"

Spring Festival

The Lunar New Year (now called the Spring Festival) falls in late January or early February and is the most important festival in modern China (as it was in the past).

Traditionally, the beginning of the New Year was considered a time for clearing up (paying off debts, spring-cleaning the house from top to bottom) in preparation for a prosperous year ahead. The first task was to make sure that the kitchen god (whose effigy or portrait stood in every house by the stove) was happy. It was believed that he went up to heaven every Spring Festival and reported on the household. If his report was good, then the gods would look after the family in the new year. Long strips of red paper with the words "When you go up to Heaven, report favourably" and "When you come back down to earth, bring good luck" were pasted on either side of the stove and the mouth of the god's effigy was smeared with honey. This was either to make sure that he would use "honeyed" words or, perhaps, to stick his mouth together so he could not say anything bad — no-one is quite sure. On the outside doors to the house pictures of fierce-looking guardian soldiers were pasted, to keep evil spirits away.

In China today, there are no kitchen gods, but the idea of spring-cleaning remains. In traditional-style houses, there is no glass in

---

COLOURS

Red is the lucky colour in China, worn at weddings and by children.

White was, traditionally, the colour of mourning. Nowadays people tend to wear a black armband, often with the single character that means "filial piety" if a parent has died, and carry a white flower made of tissue paper in funeral processions.

The entrance to a southern house. Over the door the "double happiness" symbol has been pasted up, with the character for happiness written twice. Such symbols are stuck up at the Chinese New Year or when there is a wedding in the family. Household pets are rare except in the countryside where they are kept to chase mice and rats.

PAPER-CUTS

Paper-cuts were traditionally made by peasant women, either as embroidery patterns or to use as stencils to make the white-resist patterns on the cloth which they dyed indigo blue (the common peasant cloth), or to decorate paper windows at Spring Festival. They are cut from fine paper either with scissors or, for more delicate and intricate designs, with a sharp knife. In the 1940s, when the Communists were working from their base in northwest China, at Yan'an, artists and intellectuals greatly admired the local paper-cuts and the tradition was developed into a popular art form. All over China, paper-cuts are made, either in plain colours or coloured with bright inks that are allowed to seep through the paper before it is cut.

the windows but fine white paper stuck over a wooden lattice and this window paper is renewed at Spring Festival. In some parts of China special window decorations are put up. In Hebei province red paper-cuts are stuck onto the new window paper, and in the town of Datong, in Shanxi province, hand-painted paper with flowers, birds and cats is stuck up, instead of the usual plain white paper.

Spring Festival is a national holiday, though some people have longer off work than others. It is a time when all Chinese want to be with their families and those working away from home get a few weeks leave so that they can travel home. The trains are booked up and bursting for weeks around Spring Festival. Passengers carry bundles of bedding — everyone in China travels with his two brightly coloured quilts, and no hotel in China provides bedding since it is assumed that travellers will bring it along with them — and presents for children, or local delicacies like peanuts from Shandong, dried fruit

from Beijing, tea from the Dragon Well near Hangzhou or biscuits and cakes in bright boxes.

On the day of the festival, families prepare a special meal together. One of the best things to eat is *jiaozi* — pronounced jow (as in "jowls") — tsa (as in "it's a"). These are little pastry packets of minced pork flavoured with ginger and garlic. All the family sits round a table making the *jiaozi* and joking about how many they will be able to eat (up to fifty!)

After a family meal, everyone goes to call on neighbours and friends, to drink tea and eat sweets or nuts. The side-streets and lanes are full of people going about their business at any time of the year, but at Spring Festival all you can see is families entering one courtyard after another, visiting friends. Children break the conversation by letting off fire-crackers in the courtyards. Fire-crackers are like long strings of bangers tied

◁ *Travellers carry bundles of bedding with them, as this man does by means of a yoke. There are always little stalls on station platforms selling fruit and steamed bread buns stuffed with meat.*

Making jiaozi — a New Year tradition. These girls are orphans from a school which had been hit by an earthquake, 1978.

together so that they go off one after another like machine-gun fire. In the past they were let off at Spring Festival to frighten away any lurking evil spirits.

Food

Eating is one of the highlights of the Spring Festival and one of the passions of the Chinese, who are extremely proud of their rich and varied culinary heritage. Chinese cooking varies enormously from place to place, but may be divided broadly into four regions: the north, which includes Mongolia with its winter hot-pot and the famous roast duck of Beijing; the west, where the famous food of Sichuan province is spicy and full of red chilli pepper; the east, around the mouth of the Changjiang (Yangtse) river, where fish from river or sea are cooked in delicate sauces and clear soups are full of noodles and tiny dumplings; and the south, near Guangdong province, where food is so varied as to be

△
Inside a Chinese kitchen, shared by three families.

People buy ready-prepared food which they take away in tin boxes. It would take too long to prepare the food themselves for each meal.

▽

△

The Chinese often take a long time over their midday meal. They are eating rice with meat and vegetables. Small children who have not learnt to use chopsticks either use a spoon or are fed by their parents. Here three generations eat together.

A beer and noodle parlour in Shanghai. Chinese restaurants are sparsely decorated, but serve very good food.

▽

almost unclassifiable.

A lantern shop in Beijing.

Whatever the merits of each area as far as food is concerned, all Chinese are fiercely regional in their preferences. If you tell someone from Beijing that you are going to Tianjin (about an hour away by train southeast), he will tell you that food is better in Beijing. A native of Tianjin, on the other hand, will declare that Tianjin food is the best of all and tell you what to eat and in which restaurant.

Most people have all their meals at home and this presents a problem since Chinese food takes time to prepare. All the vegeta-bles and meat need to be chopped into tiny, chopstick-size pieces. As the Chinese prefer fresh ingredients but do not yet have fridges, someone must buy fresh food at least once a day and then spend a long time chopping it up. Most people, in city and countryside, live in three-generation family units, and so it is often the retired grandparents who do the shopping and cooking and mind the small children while others are out at work. There are ways of saving time, for most

16

people have good canteens at work and can eat there or fill a tin food box to take home. Many people live in housing built around their workplace, and their children, too, can eat in the canteen if their parents are at work. In cities little shops sell ready-minced pork or steamed bread which takes some of the time out of preparing a meal.

Perhaps because cooking is such a lengthy process and ties one person to the stove right through the meal, birthdays, weddings and special events are often celebrated in restaurants. In the major cities there are restaurants serving food from all the provinces, and in cities like Shanghai, Tianjin and Beijing, which used to have large foreign populations, there are western food restaurants as well. In all the suburbs and small towns there are plenty of restaurants, which, though not smartly decorated, serve very good food. All you will see are plain walls, wooden tables and stools, simple white bowls, rather bent bamboo chopsticks or red enamel spoons and a blackboard with the menu chalked up. The names of Chinese dishes are pretty but not very helpful: "Braised four treasures"

means braised duck webs, duck wings, duck tongues and duck kidneys; "Plum blossom and snow competing for spring" means apples and bananas in a sort of custard; "Ants climbing trees" is a lovely Sichuan dish of minced pork, chilli and rice noodles; and "Silk thread apples" describes toffee apples where the stray strands of toffee look like fine silk threads.

The Lantern Festival

About two weeks after Spring Festival there is the lantern festival. This used to be another occasion for fire-crackers — possibly with the original intention of encouraging spring rains to help the growth of early crops. Today, although you can still hear the odd fire-cracker (left over from Spring Festival), children put most of their energy into persuading their parents to buy them coloured paper lanterns. Shaped like goldfish or birds or simply great round red globes, these lanterns are lit with a small candle and carried through the streets. Great glowing red circles bob about in the cold dark winter night.

March

"Waking of insects; spring equinox"

In north China March is the beginning of the growing season. Though it is still cold, the heavy frosts are over and ploughing and planting can begin. In the warm south the agricultural season is well under way.

"Women hold up half the sky"

8 March is an international women's day, not a traditional Chinese festival, but it is a

celebration that is particularly important in the socialist countries. It is not a holiday, though many women may have time off work to go to meetings which are held throughout the country, presided over by remarkable women and attended only by women. In Shanghai, Song Qingling, widow of Sun Yatsen (1866-1925), founder of the Guomindang Party and the leader of the 1911 revolt against the last dynasty, might preside

17

over a meeting and in Beijing, Deng Ying-chao, widow of Zhou Enlai (1898-1976), might address a meeting of thousands of women in the Great Hall of the People. Both these women are known through their husbands but are also famous in their own right.

As the newspaper editorials on 8 March point out, the position of women in China is infinitely better than it was in the past, even as recently as the first part of the twentieth century. According to the traditional system of belief, based partly on the ideas of Confucius (c.551 BC-c.479 BC), a political advisor to feudal rulers, order in the state depended on people keeping in their places and respecting the authority given by heaven to the ruler. It was right that the subject obey his ruler, a son obey

The blossom begins to bloom in March. The Chinese have a great reverence for nature.

his father and wife obey both her husband and her grown-up sons. The woman was right at the bottom of the chain of command. Girls were married by their parents who arranged the contract with the husband's parents, neither side consulting the young people. This was not so hard for the man, for he could respectably take other wives if he did not like the first one or she did not provide him with a son. As long as he could afford them, he could have several extra wives and could stay out drinking in the company of friends and singing girls. Women, however, were expected to remain absolutely faithful, no matter how awful their husband, and it was a total disgrace to divorce or even

18

THE BALLAD OF MULAN

Mulan was a girl who lived in the fifth century. When her elderly father was called up to go to war, she went in his place, since the family's honour depended upon someone answering the Emperor's demand. Mulan is a very popular figure in both poetry and paintings.

Heaving sigh after sigh,
Mulan sits weaving in the doorway.
Are you thinking of your love?
Are you sighing for your love?
I have no lover,
I am not sighing for a lover.
Last night I read the battle roll:
The great Khan is calling up his soldiers,
Their names in lists on twelve long scrolls.
My father's name is on each scroll.
My father has no grown son.
Mulan has no elder brother.
I will go to the city to buy a saddle and a horse
And go to battle in my father's place.
In the Eastern market she bought a piebald horse
In the Western market she bought a saddle and a
    blanket
In the Southern market she bought a bridle
And in the Northern market she bought a long
    whip.
At dawn she said goodbye to her father and
    mother
At dusk she pitched camp on the banks of the
    Yellow River . . .
The winter sun gleamed on her iron armour . . .
After a hundred battles the [enemy] general was
    killed
After ten years the warriors could return
    home . . .
I opened the door to the Eastern apartments
I sat on my bed in the Western apartments.
I took off my soldier's robe and put on the dress
    I used to wear.
At the window I piled up my cloudy hair
At the mirror I put on my make-up.
At the gate I met my fellow-soldiers who were
    shocked to see me
For we had served together for ten years but
    they didn't know Mulan was a girl.
The male hare tucks its feet in when it sits
A female hare is recognized by her cloudy eyes.
But when they are running side by side,
Who can tell which is which?

*(shortened translation of the anonymous
ballad of the Six Dynasties period,
317–589 AD)*

to re-marry on the death of the husband. The most virtuous thing a widow could do was to commit suicide and the streets of old China were criss-crossed with memorial arches (called *pailou*), erected to commemorate virtuous suicidal widows. When a girl married she became the property of her husband's family and could only visit her parents' home after the birth of a son. A man, on the other hand, was not expected to break with his family, for his new wife became a member of his father's household.

Footbinding

Particularly at the beginning of the twentieth century, when western ideas of free choice and love were gradually spreading in China, women began to react against traditional ways. One of the greatest struggles was against footbinding which was considered essential if a girl was to attract a good husband, since no-one wanted a girl with "big" (in other words normal-sized) feet. From about the age of five, little girls' feet were wrapped tightly in cotton bandages, bending the toes under the sole of the foot to create the tiny "lily feet" that were much admired. In fact, they looked more like horses' hoofs and the process of breaking the toes under the foot was terribly painful; it was also bad for the circulation in the legs, restricted the girl's freedom of movement and condemned her to a life of bandaged feet since, once deformed, the feet required the bandages as support so that the girl could hobble about. The custom seems to have begun during the Song dynasty (960-1297), when an Emperor had a favourite concubine with tiny feet who started a fashion. Though it seems appalling to us, the Chinese were quite surprised when Victorian missionary ladies from Britain protested, for, to the Chinese, it was unhealthy and barbaric to squash the waist into figure-deforming corsets.

At the beginning of the twentieth century, when girls were beginning to resist footbinding and refuse arranged marriage, they

A bride and groom have their photograph taken in Shanghai, 1980. The wedding clothes are the photographer's props.

had, as Mao Zedong (Mao Tse tung) wrote in 1919, very little alternative. It was not at all respectable for a woman to work and earn her living, and so girls were dependent upon their parents or their husbands to survive. The impossibility of the position sometimes led to tragedy, when a girl cut her throat in the bridal sedan-chair, unable to go through with the ceremony but equally unable to see a future for herself otherwise.

In 1949, when the Communist Party came to power, the first pieces of legislation passed were intended to improve the position of women. The new Land Law gave them equal right to hold land, which meant that a woman could support herself. The Marriage Law made arranged marriages practically impossible, since both partners must now assure the magistrate that they are marrying of their own free will. Divorce is no longer a disgrace for a woman, although it is still comparatively rare because divorce courts make a determined effort to reconcile husband and wife and only grant a divorce when they have seen a reconciliation to be impossible.

Population Control

China's population has passed 100 million and the government is trying very hard to control population growth. Late marriage at about 25 for women and 27 for men, or later, is encouraged and couples should not have more than two, widely spaced children. Quite drastic measures have been taken to enforce these recommendations, although they are always expressed in terms of the greater good. People must see themselves as part of a larger group, with responsibility to others, and must realize that if they have large families, the strain they place on local

A generation apart. The girl has been reading to her grandmother, who cannot read, and she is now practising arithmetic on her abacus. The old lady's feet were obviously bound when she was young.

20

resources is detrimental to the well-being of others.

Every work-place and district in a city and every commune in the countryside has its own birth control programme. If a couple has no children or their first child is three years old, they are allowed to have a baby, but if they already have two children or a first child under three, they are actively discouraged. In effect, in each place where there is a birth control unit with a planned schedule of growth, everyone knows whose turn it is to have a baby this year!

Recently, the government has also introduced financial incentives for the one-child family. If a couple with one child sign a declaration that they will have no more children, they receive a little extra money per month plus free health and kindergarten care for their one child. That child is also guaranteed a good chance of secondary and higher education. Parents who have a third child have the same amount of money docked from their wages and have to pay kindergarten and health care fees for that child.

Kites

Spring in north China is very windy, which makes life uncomfortable for the millions of cyclists but exciting for kite fliers. Kites have been made in China for centuries. One of the first kite stories is that of General Han Xin who in 100 BC flew a kite over the walls of a city he was besieging so that he could calculate trigonometrically the length of a tunnel that he was secretly digging under the ramparts. Boys used to stick powdered glass onto their kite strings and fight with kites, each trying to break the other's kite string. Today you can see kites made from thin paper pasted over a light bamboo frame to form birds, butterflies, grasshoppers, sometimes with round bodies and separate legs. Or there are long dragon kites made of many segments which twist and turn in the air. Many of the finest kites are family heirlooms, only flown with great care on rare and perfect days. Others are home-made from sheets of newspaper, with newspaper tails, and no-one minds if they get stuck in trees.

Dust Storms

Another effect of the spring winds in the north is that they occasionally whip up dust storms. These used to be very common, so much so that people wrapped their best possessions in blue cloth even if they were to be put away in chests, for the fine dust would creep in around window frames and into locked boxes. Now that much of the north has been re-planted with trees, dust storms are rare, but when they come they are dramatic. The sky fills with a fine gritty dust which gets into everything and grates on the teeth. It gets dark in a sinister yellow way, early in the afternoon, and small children have their faces wrapped in chiffon scarves to protect them. The storms only last a day or so but are a strong reminder of the nearness of the Gobi desert from which the dust is blown.

The Summer Palace

Despite the occasional dust storm, spring is a time of increasing sun and flowers. Like their neighbours the Japanese, the Chinese have a great reverence for nature and for the flowers that mark the changes of the seasons. In early spring the plum blossom that covers the slopes of Longevity Hill at the Summer Palace makes a trip out to the northwestern suburbs of Beijing worthwhile.

The Summer Palace was built for the imperial family so that they could pass the summer in the cool foothills of the mountains which rise to the Mongolian plateau. (The city of Beijing on the plain gets terribly hot and humid in mid-summer.) The site was developed by Emperors throughout the centuries: the twelfth-century "Garden of Golden Waters" became the "Garden of Wonderful Hills" during the Ming dynasty

A visitor to the Great Wall covers her head with a piece of chiffon against the wind and dust.

A boat trip on the lake of the Summer Palace.

A young visitor in the courtyard of the Summer Palace. Seasonal flowers are grown in pots and brought out when they bloom.

(1368-1644), but it was the Qianlong Emperor of the Qing who carried out the most extensive work there to honour his mother's sixtieth birthday in the mid-eighteenth century. He constructed many little gardens to resemble those of the southern cities of Hangzhou and Wuxi that she loved, and since it was in honour of her birthday, many of the pavilions and hills have appropriate names: "Hill of Longevity", "Palace of Joy and Longevity", "Hall of Goodness and Longevity".

Like many of the fine imperial buildings of the Qing dynasty (1644-1911), the Summer Palace was twice damaged by western armies — in 1860, as a result of the Opium War, and again in 1900, as a reprisal for the Boxer Uprising, which had resulted in the deaths of some foreigners and the siege of the foreign embassies in Beijing. Both times the Palace had to be re-built. Today it is one of Beijing's most beautiful parks, most noted for its garden architecture and for the flowers that flourish there, beginning with the plum blossom.

A covered walk in the Summer Palace gardens.

April

"Pure brightness; corn rain"

Qing Ming Festival – Honouring the Dead

In April (though sometimes in March because of the movement of the lunar New Year)

the Qing Ming or Clear and Bright Festival occurs, when living Chinese honour their ancestors. You can still see some people in China (and lots of people in Hong Kong) going out to their ancestors' graves, sweeping them, weeding them and setting up a picnic

At one Qing Ming festival, children at the Monument to Revolutionary Martyrs in the centre of Beijing take a pledge to be good successors to the revolutionary cause. In the background is one of the gates in the old city wall.

In Shanghai brightly coloured paper funeral wreaths are carried on long poles by the wreath-makers.

with joss sticks burning in front of the tombs.

In modern China the Qing Ming festival has officially become a day to honour "collective ancestors", those who fought and died for the revolution and against oppression in the past. Instead of going to the family graves, schoolchildren are taken to monuments to the martyrs of the revolution and told of their brave deeds. They perhaps lay a small wreath. Over the last few years, the Qing Ming festival has become very important for, since the great heroes of the war of

liberation have almost all died recently, there is a real sense of the need to remember them. In 1976, a few months after the death of Premier Zhou Enlai, a man who had been intimately associated with modern China's achievements, the people of Beijing crowded into the Square of Heavenly Peace to pile their wreaths of bright paper flowers around the monument to the martyrs of the revolution. The city authorities were worried by this spontaneous gathering of thousands of people and tried to remove the wreaths and disperse the crowd, but this provoked a riot. In the years since then, there has been no attempt to limit the expression

Ancestors' graves are being slowly moved from farming land, near Guangzhou. In some parts of southern China, secondary burial is common. A few years after burial, the bones are dug up and then kept in pottery jars.

of respect for such leaders as Zhou Enlai at the Qing Ming festival.

Chinese funerary practices spring from a system of belief which treats the spirit of a dead person rather like a living person who needs food, clothing and material comfort in order to remain happy and friendly. Beliefs about the afterworld and what happens to the spirit after death go back thousands of years and have not changed drastically since the fifth century BC.

The Chinese believed (and some still do) that after death, the spirit hung around for a few days before beginning its journey to the other world, where life was an equivalent of that lived on earth. Funerary customs, therefore, had to comfort the spirit in those first few days (in case it turned nasty), providing it first with food and clothing, then with things it would need on the journey (money, a horse, shoes) and, finally, with what it would need in the spirit world. In the past real sacrifices were made in the grave to accompany the spirits of the Kings of the Shang dynasty (c.1600 BC - 1027 BC): chariots, complete with horses and charioteers, were buried around the royal coffin. Later these were replaced with pottery models of farms, pigs in their pens, warriors on horseback and whole orchestras of court

27

CONFUCIUS

Confucius did not start "ancestor worship" in China, but, as with so many other things, he spoke about it, his words were written down and, as he gradually became venerated, his ideas on the subject were followed very carefully.

Confucius lived between about 551 BC and 459 BC. Though he spent much time out of work, he acted as an advisor on affairs of state to some of the rulers of the "Warring States" period (so called because China was for some centuries divided into seven separate states who fought each other until one beat all the others, unifying China in 221 BC). His concern was the smooth running of the state, and he believed this to result from a maintenance of order. Within the family, just as in the state, there had to be a hierarchy and it was important that everyone knew his or her place and kept to it. The state-family hierarchy of obedience had the ruler at the top who was to be obeyed by his subjects, the father of a family in the middle (obeyed by his son and his wife) and the wife at the very bottom. Within the family, age was to be respected, and the recently dead were almost as important. The names of dead ancestors were written on tablets to be kept on the family altar and they "joined in" all sorts of family festivities and events. Confucius stressed the importance of "filial piety" – a concept which has given rise since to many odd stories about children who looked after their elderly parents very well. Girls were praised for lying naked on the snow to melt a little water for their parents to drink, and there is a strange tale of a man who played like a baby to amuse his very elderly parents.

Most of Confucius's pearls of wisdom took the form of little stories which were recorded by disciples, like the one about the Master (Confucius) travelling through Shandong province in a cart. He met a woman who was weeping bitterly and he leaned out of the cart to ask her what was the matter? She told him that her husband, her uncle and now her son had all been killed by a tiger. (Tigers were not unknown in northern China at the time though they have since retreated much further north towards Siberia.) Confucius asked her why she did not move away since tigers were such a threat in the neighbourhood and she replied that there was a good ruler. The Master turned to his disciples and said: "You see? Bad government is worse than a tiger."

musicians. By about the tenth century AD these ceramic models were, in turn, increasingly replaced with paper models. This meant that funerals were cheaper. Paper models for funerals are still made and sold in the street markets of Hong Kong. They show how the Chinese approach to life after death and its requirements has evolved but not changed, for now, instead of horses, there are aeroplanes and sports cars among the models of houses and servants.

All these paper models are burnt at the funeral so that they can accompany the spirit "in essence", and at the Qing Ming festival paper shoes, clothes and money are burnt at the tomb. The offerings of food made to the ancestors, bowls of rice, whole roasted chickens, dishes of cooked vegetables, are also eaten "in essence" by the spirit, after which the family sit and eat the picnic in front of the tomb.

The importance of ancestors to the Chinese dates back at least as far as the Shang dynasty (c.1600 BC-1027 BC), when the imperial ancestors were questioned about important affairs of state. Oracles used to write the question on an ox shoulderblade or on a tortoise shell. Heat was then applied to the bone or shell, and the ancestor's answer was read in the cracks that appeared. These "oracle bones" are the first example of Chinese writing and they show that, at

All Chinese characters, whether they consist of only two strokes or up to twenty-two, use a combination of the following eight basic strokes:

、　　　　　dot

一　　　　　horizontal line which must be written from left to right

丨　　　　　vertical line — must be written from top to bottom

丿乀　　　　left-falling and right-falling which are written from top to bottom

㇓　　　　　rising; this one is written from bottom to top

亅乚乚乚　　hooks; all are written from top to bottom

㇆乛㇆　　　horizontal hooks, written from left (top) to right (bottom)

Try writing out the following phrases, remembering also that within each character, the left-hand part is written before the right-hand section, or, if a character is one that consists of a bottom part and a top part (as in míngzi), the top must be written before the bottom.

你　好！ Nǐ hǎo! (How are you?) *phonetic pronunciation:* Nee How?

你　早！ Nǐ zǎo! (Good morning.) *phonetic pronunciation:* Nee dzow

你　叫　什么　名字？ Nǐ jiào shénme míngzi? (What is your name?) *phonetic pronunciation:*
Nee jow (as in jowl) shernmo mingtzer?

我　叫 Wǒ jiào . . . . . . (My name is . . . .) *phonetic pronunciation:* War (as in warm) jow . . .

再　见！ Zài jiàn! (See you again.) *phonetic pronunciation:* Dzeye (as in eye) jen (as in Jennifer)

The little marks over the romanisation are important. They indicate tones and you should try to make your voice rise or fall in the direction indicated, otherwise Chinese people would find you hard to understand.

that early period, the Chinese were already beginning to write in vertical (rather than horizontal) lines, and from right to left.

Chinese Script

The Chinese script, which is first found on the Shang "oracle bones", is different from all others in that it has remained non-alphabetic. Many scripts started as the Chinese did, with pictures representing separate things, but only the Chinese have continued to develop their script on this basis. Obviously, they do not still draw pictures, for they would not be able to express complex ideas in that way, but their "characters" have become ideographic (they represent an idea rather than a picture) and are fascinating in

their intricate construction.

The Chinese written language consists of many thousands of separate characters; the average vocabulary of an educated Chinese in the past was 7,000 to 8,000 characters. Each character is different, each represents a different word without necessarily giving any indication of how the word is pronounced, and each may be written with up to twenty strokes.

It is widely known that there are many different regional dialects in China and that a person from Beijing could not understand a person from Guangzhou (Canton). However, the writing system is a unifying factor. Since it conveys what a word means (rather than how it sounds), it can be understood by those who speak different dialects.

The enormous number of characters, each of which has to be separately learnt, presents quite a task to the schoolchild. The way that characters are taught reflects the separation of the written and the spoken language. Children first learn the Roman

Chinese script. The girl is copying a poem about Hua Guofeng.

Waiting outside the cinema. The film is one that was popular in the Cultural Revolution period, Taking Tiger Mountain by Strategy, a "modern revolutionary Peking opera".

alphabet and group characters according to pronunciation.

In the past, it was sufficient that written communication was understood throughout the country. But in the era of radio, television and cinema, the Chinese government has had to ensure that a common spoken language can be understood by everyone in China. In 1956 *putonghua* or "common language" was introduced as the official language of instruction in schools and the national broadcast media. *Putonghua* is basically the dialect of the north, which is spoken by four fifths of the population (with minor variations) anyway. Where it is not the local dialect, it is taught in schools at the same time as the written system when children learn the Roman alphabet with its sound values for *putonghua*. In 1956 adults were mostly taught the new "common language" in evening classes, but there are still some old people who did not pick it up, because of their age or because they were living in remote areas.

"Beginning of summer; grain full"

May Day

The first of May is one of China's rare holidays. It is not a traditional holiday but, as International Worker's Day, it is a modern socialist holiday. Everyone in China has the day off to celebrate and, since there is no traditional way of celebrating, the festivities are organized by the state. All the parks in every city are decorated. In the north there may still be peonies in flower. These are one of the favourite flowers of China, the symbol of spring (as the lotus symbolizes summer, plum blossom winter and the chrysanthemum, autumn), also called "the flower of riches and honour". The bark of the peony root is used in traditional Chinese herbal medicine, to treat blood disorders, and it was said that a peony plant could indicate family fortune. If the flower flourished, then so would its owner, but if the leaves withered and the flowers dropped prematurely, the change presaged poverty or some overwhelming disaster.

Peonies are nearly over by May and there is often little blossom left in the trees and so the people decorating the parks may have to help nature by tying tiny pink tissue-paper flowers all over the trees along the lake and wiring paper flowers onto the green stems of tree peonies that have finished flowering. In the ponds at the Summer Palace in Beijing, plastic lotus flowers float, anticipating August when real lotus flowers appear. Apart from the paper and real flowers, there are fairground booths where you can test your aim with an airgun, fruit stalls, toy stalls, where you can buy little presents for children, and biscuit stalls, where you can buy something to nibble as you walk through the park.

Visitors to the parks on May Day are admitted by tickets issued through their place of work, and they may get a chance to go once every three years or so. In the parks they can see giant display games of Chinese chess, played between experts under a huge board which stands like a hoarding behind them. The pieces are hung up in the appro-

A national dance under the trees decorated with paper flowers on May Day, Beijing, 1973.

A firework display in Tien an Men Square, Beijing, ▷
at the end of the May Day celebrations.

priate places so that the audience can follow their moves. There are also lots of different open-air stage performances in which the colourful dresses and exuberant dances of China's minorities are dominant. The Chinese have sometimes found it difficult to assimilate their own traditional culture into modern entertainment, for much of the traditional local opera (very lengthy mixtures of singing and acrobatics) is terribly hard to understand, but the folk dances and brilliant costumes of the minorities are easily accessible.

In the evening there are gigantic firework displays over the cities. Fireworks have been made in China for many centuries, ever since the discovery of gunpowder at the end of the ninth century AD. At that time alchemists experimenting with explosive mixtures were warned to beware, since accidents had occurred where the alchemist's beard had been singed and the buildings in which he was working had burned down. Gunpowder was used in weapons of all sorts in China well before it was known either to the Arabs or in the west, but it was also used to make beautiful fireworks. Fireworks are called "flower explosions" in Chinese, while firecrackers (like bangers) are called "exploding bamboo" and are wrapped in paper made from bamboo.

The Dragon Boat Festival

The best-known traditional festival in May, the Dragon Boat Festival, is celebrated throughout China but especially in the south.

32

In Hong Kong today you can still watch races between long boats decorated as dragons. In the north people eat sticky rice cakes. These are made with glutinous rice and sweet dates, wrapped in leaves and steamed, and are eaten with sugar. Both the boat races and the glutinous rice cakes are connected with the suicide of the honest politician (and poet) Qu Yuan. In about 288 BC he threw himself into a river in protest against corruption in the government. As he was greatly respected, the local people threw rice into the water for the fish to eat so that they would not eat Qu Yuan's body. The Chinese believed that it was important for a body to remain whole, for otherwise the spirit would spend its time wandering unhappily looking for the lost parts. For this reason, the worst and most disgraceful form of capital punishment was beheading, which would leave the soul divided and unhappy. Hanging and strangulation were reserved for less awful crimes.

The boat races in Hong Kong may have their origin in a search for Qu Yuan's body, but they also recall the Chinese belief that dragons live in rivers and lakes and are responsible for rainfall. Drought meant disaster for the peasants who would not be able to pay their taxes which were collected in the form of rice. The government suffered if it could not collect its revenue, and so during droughts local government officials would go to river banks and throw offerings of food to placate the angry dragons and plead for rain.

33

NATIONAL MINORITIES IN CHINA

94 per cent of the population of China are ethnic Chinese, who call themselves "Han" people. The rest of the population consists of people who are culturally and, in some cases, racially distinct from the Hans. There are 54 different "minorities" in China, ranging from the Tibetans, to the Manchus (who ruled China from 1644-1911), the Mongols (who ruled from 1279-1368) and the Turkic Uighurs. Along the southern border with Burma there are Zhuang and Miao, and near the Korean border there are Koreans.

That these peoples are part of China is rarely disputed, for throughout China's history her spread of influence and power has been huge (except during brief periods of imperial decline). Since 1949 the government policy towards minorities has been to encourage cultural and linguistic continuity in minority areas, while bringing them politically and economically into a position consistent with the aims of the central government. Many of the minority peoples live in "autonomous areas" where, as stated, it is mainly in cultural affairs that there is real autonomy. In some respects there is different treatment for minorities. For example, they are mostly exempted from the strict family planning programmes, since their birth-rates have tended to decline, and they are now encouraged to increase their population.

There is sometimes a slightly uneasy relationship between the Hans and the minorities, who are usually distinctively

In Mongolia the basic method of transport is the horse. Raising livestock is Mongolia's basic industry, as the country is generally too infertile for crops.

dressed in national costume and may therefore be treated as "quaint". This is increased by the frequent reliance on the colourful national dances and songs of the minority peoples for entertainment at National Day and May Day celebrations. For such a small percentage of the population, the minorities offer much in the way of entertainment, but clearly they have more to offer than that. Many of them have rich cultural backgrounds and strong religious heritages (the Muslim Uighurs, the Lamaist Mongolians and Tibetans, for instance), which are beginning to recover from the suppression of the Cultural Revolution.

Xinjiang Uighur carpet makers.

Map showing minorities.

35

June

"Grain in the ear; summer solstice"

In the hot month of June crickets whirr in all the trees. Small boys throw sticks into the branches to dislodge the crickets which they then keep in tiny wicker cages. For centuries crickets have been kept as pets in China, their little cages furnished with porcelain bowls for water and food. In the past, street vendors sold crickets costing almost nothing in June and it was wise to buy then, because in the autumn, when they had to be artificially reared, they might cost a thousand times as much. Most people kept their crickets in bamboo or wicker cages, but some spent small fortunes on porcelain cages made in the imperial factories and even more for porcelain water-bowls. Some crickets were kept for their "song" (the loud whirring noise), others were prized as fighters and were entered in contests. There are hundreds of different varieties of cricket, as you can see if you look for them in the trees or in the long grass at the Ming tombs outside Beijing. They have different names according to their appearance: white-spotted heads, crab-shell greens, lute-wings, plum-flower wings or bamboo-joint whiskers.

Pets

Other popular pets in China today are goldfish and cage birds. Cats and dogs exist as hunting or working animals, keeping down mice and rats. Dogs are kept especially in south China where they help in hunting, but are also eaten as a delicacy. Since there are not many "domestic" cats, there is a cage full of them in the Nanjing Zoo. Though they are, to us, ordinary tabbies and marmalade cats, they are nearly as interesting as pandas to the Chinese visitors. The reason for the small number of cats and dogs as pets is that, in the 1950s when China was desperately short of food for people, domestic pets in the cities were rounded up and destroyed because they were eating food that was needed by hungry people. Since then smaller and less greedy pets have continued to be popular in their place. All sorts of little song birds are kept and cared for. In summer you can see their cages hung out in the fresh air and old men take their birds in their

A goldfish seller.

cages for a walk, or even for a bicycle ride.

Goldfish are almost a national hobby. In China they exist in as many different shapes, sizes and colours as dogs in England. There are black ones, gold ones, white ones, striped, spotted and patched ones, ones with simple tails or tails as soft as a swatch of silk floating behind them, and some have pop-eyes like Pekinese dogs. While they are popular pets, they are also important features of many of the parks in China. In Hangzhou there are several pools around a lake, each with different carp, great golden ones, smaller white ones or huge grey ones which rise quietly out of the green water like sharks if they see a crumb of bread on the surface. Nearby, at the Jade Spring, especially magnificent goldfish are exhibited to the public, each specimen swimming in a great porcelain or stoneware bowl with dragons painted on it. Nowadays these displays of goldfish are

A mother buys a hat for her daughter at a children's store in Shanghai.

often publicly organized, but in the past every private household in Beijing would have a big bowl of goldfish in the courtyard, between flowering pomegranates and oleanders. The custom was so common that the local saying, "a mat covering overhead [to provide shade from the hot sun], an earthenware fish-jar and a flowering pomegranate tree" was not a pleasant description of June in the capital but was used as a criticism of uniformity.

Children's Day

1 June is a national holiday for children only. There are special performances of puppet shows or films for children and many

37

"Tiger shoes".

Ping pong, the "national sport" in China. Simple tables are put up anywhere. In winter the game is played indoors.

schoolchildren go out with their teachers into the sunny parks. Otherwise, it is unlikely that children will get presents, for they have rather few toys. They get toys at Spring Festival, and when the family goes out somewhere special, a child might get a small souvenir, but, in general, there is not a great choice of toys in the shops and people do not have enough money to buy many.

Babies have home-made soft toys, little yellow tigers with furry whiskers and the character for "king" embroidered on their foreheads. The same tigers occur on babies' clothes. They often have "tiger shoes", which have stuffed and embroidered tiger faces on the toes, with thread whiskers and cloth ears. Hats for babies have an embroidered tiger face and fur-trimmed cloth ears. Both tiger hats and tiger shoes spring from traditional ideas of protecting children against evil spirits which might be scared away by the sight of a tiger. In traditional China

sons were especially precious, as they would not marry and leave the family but would stay to look after their parents in old age. They were considered as being especially vulnerable to evil spirits. Since it was believed that evil spirits could not really be bothered to carry off girl babies, some parents would pierce the ears of their baby sons and give them ear-rings to confuse evil spirits into thinking that the child was a girl.

Older children have guns and dolls, but they are less common than in the west. Children mostly play out of doors at football, badminton or ping pong or at traditional games like "foot shuttlecock". This is played by any number and requires only a shuttlecock, which is made of a small bean bag with feathers tied at one end. The aim is to kick it to each other and not to let it fall to the ground. The skilful can keep the shuttlecock in the air by kicking it with the side of the heel as well as with the toe.

July

"Slight heat; great heat"

Summer Clothes

Practically all the annual rainfall in China falls in the months of July and August when the temperature is in the 20s and 30s Centigrade and the humidity is about 90 degrees. After heavy, thundery days, great torrents of rain come as a relief but mean that summer wear in China must always include some rain-proof covering. In summer, men wear a light pair of trousers and a cotton shirt for work or a bright vest for Sundays, covered

with a long, hooded mackintosh and wellington boots. Underneath their rain wear, women may wear trousers and a blouse or perhaps a skirt or dress in bright, flowered cotton with light plastic sandals (which are all right in the rain). Boys wear light cotton shorts or trousers, and little girls wear dresses. In the countryside, children wear practically nothing in the hottest months, sometimes just a little apron in front and a pair of luminous pink plastic sandals.

In summer you find great oiled-paper umbrellas appearing in the shops. These

Guangzhou, known in the west as Canton, is a city with a long history of relations with the outside world. Situated on the mouth of the Pearl River, in the coastal province of Guangdong, it has been a trading city for centuries. From Guangdong and from the other major southern coastal province of Fujian, many Chinese have set off to the outside world to seek their fortunes and settle in Southeast Asia and further west in California, in Australia and throughout the world.

The province is fertile and sub-tropical, enabling double-cropping of rice and even treble-cropping on Hainan Island. It is warm enough to allow agricultural work throughout the year, producing sugarcane, silk, sweet potatoes, tobacco, jute, tropical fruits, like bananas, mangoes and lychees, as well as livestock (there is much fish-farming in the Pearl Delta), coffee, coconuts and rubber.

Canton is best known in the west as the first port open to the foreign traders who began to arrive from Europe in the sixteenth century. At first, the Qing government managed to restrict foreigners to the shoreline at Canton, but they were greedy to get further. European government missions, such as that of Lord Macartney from Britain in 1792, tried to open China to trade but found that since the Chinese were accustomed to dominate East Asia, they would only allow trade on the basis of superiority. Japanese, Burmese, Thai and Korean government envoys had always "kowtowed" to the Chinese Emperor, but Lord Macartney refused to knock his head on the ground three times. Unaware of the growing superiority of western arms, the Chinese continued to ignore western traders until, in the middle of the nineteenth century, they were forced to admit their demands.

The Opium Wars (1840-42, 1856) are an example of the lengths to which the west was prepared to go in order to develop its own wealth in trade. Opium was grown in India and exported to China, where millions of people gradually became dependent on the drug. India being under British rule, the British encouraged the demand for opium. They also developed tea production in India to combat the Chinese export of tea upon which Europe had come to depend.

Guangdong Province is richly fertile.

A sailing junk and other boats on the Pearl River, Guangzhou.

It was in Canton that the Chinese Opium Commissioner, Lin Zexu, took decisive action against the opium trade by burning a whole consignment at the port. The British then declared war, a war which ended in defeat for China. This meant that the British could demand the opening of China to western trade. Canton remained one of the foremost centres of China's external trade throughout the next hundred years.

From 1957 most of China's trade has been carried out through the twice-yearly trade fair held in the Canton Exhibition Centre. The fact that all foreigners were then expected to deal at the fair and that officials of the state export organizations came down from Beijing to Canton was perhaps a deliberately ironic move, for it seemed to imply that China had reversed the conditions imposed by the Opium War and was re-imposing her will on foreign traders. Since 1979, however, trade with foreign countries has been conducted on a provincial and factory basis, in a more direct way than through the Canton Fair.

As Canton is a southern city, warm throughout much of the year, people spend much time in the evenings sitting out on the street on little bamboo stools, some playing cards under the street lamps, some doing the washing, others with babies on their laps or fanning themselves.

Chinese products at the Canton Trade Fair, where goods intended for export are displayed.

The pedicab is a popular form of transport in Guangzhou. The fare is paid before the journey begins. The family sewing machine is being transported across the Pearl River. Sewing machines are important items of household possession and, like bicycles or radios, will take a long time to save up for.

41

are made with bamboo handles and oiled paper, sometimes painted with delicate birds on sprays of flowering plum, or misty mountain landscapes. They serve as both umbrella and parasol, the dual function characterizing the hot, wet summer in China.

Fruit

There are compensations for the wet weather, for summer fruits and vegetables are plentiful and varied. Lychees appear in Beijing for a couple of weeks, sent up from sub-tropical Guangzhou (Canton), an annual exception to the rule that food should be locally produced. Fresh lychees look very pretty with their scaly pink skins, soft, perfumed flesh and shiny stones, and people queue up for them when they see them on the vegetable stall. Apart from the exotic lychees, there are tomatoes, all sorts of different aubergines, from white and mauve striped to deep purple, peas, beans, strawberries, Chinese peaches (unripe-looking, pale-greeny-pink, with white flesh and a little point making them almost heart-shaped), and, above all, watermelons. Watermelon slices are sold on the streets, like ice-lollies in Britain, and beside every stall there is a bin for the skin. The skins are afterwards taken out to the countryside as pig-food.

Western-style clothes were noticeable in China in 1980.

One traditional and one more modern cape against the summer rain.

42

Two small girls in typically unironed clothing.

So, the town-dweller who eats his water-melon slice is feeding the pigs that are being reared to feed him. City-people in China have been kept quite closely in touch with the countryside, although this is gradually beginning to change. At the moment, because food is grown locally, the agricultural seasons are clear, even to town-dwellers, and the fact that all the city vegetable refuse is taken away for pig-food is another reminder of agriculture.

Hygiene

It is not only melon skins that are collected. In most of China's old cities, there is little mains drainage yet and in the little low courtyard houses, it is rare to find even running water. People use stand pipes set up along the lanes to wash their clothes and vegetables and they carry water home for washing themselves and cooking. They go to public bath-houses to wash themselves every week, and use public lavatories which are set every couple of hundred yards along the lanes. These are emptied every day into "honey-carts" — an ironic name for the little tanks pulled by mules or horses which carry the manure out of the city to the countryside, where it is stored (until any harmful bacteria have been naturally destroyed) and then used as a cheap, organic fertilizer.

Summer Sports

The Chinese are not very fond of cold water, either to drink (they think it is bad for you and prefer to drink very hot water) or to swim in, and so it is not until July that many people are to be seen in the lakes and ponds. In July the moat around the Forbidden City, used as a skating rink in winter, becomes a central swimming pool. Kunming Lake at the Summer Palace is also used for both these sports (with changing rooms in one of the Old Palace outhouses).

Other favourite summer sports are basketball, volleyball and ping pong. Ping pong must be considered the national sport of China; even tiny children play it really well. In winter it is a practical indoor exercise, but in summer it is a game for all, since there are simple tables (built of bricks and concrete with a row of bricks for a net) everywhere: in parks, between blocks of flats on housing estates, in school recreation grounds and at sports centres.

Children who show a special aptitude for sports may be given training in the "spare-time schools" or "Children's Palaces" in every town. Children's Palace is the name given to a neighbourhood centre where children of school-age can go after school. Most of them will have working parents who are unable to get home till later in the afternoon. At the Children's Palace the children can play in a safe area with some simple facilities or join others in specialized activities. Children's Palaces tend to sound like bedlam, for there are noisy sporting activities outside,

43

and inside the building there may be violin, accordion, piano, ballet, choral singing and orchestral classes, as well as painting, foreign language, paper-cut and writing classes.

Children who show talent for a particular subject, particularly in sports, may be sent from the Children's Palace to a "spare-time school". These, again, are organized in all the cities and exist to train sportsmen and women, after school or work. Perhaps one of the most interesting sporting activities in China, and one which figures largely in "spare-time schools" is *wu shu* or the martial arts.

The Martial Arts

The martial arts are quite well-known, though badly represented, through the Hong Kong "kung fu" films. There are hundreds of different kinds of martial art in China, ranging from the slow, balletic exercise system, *tai ji quan*, to fast, acrobatic swordplay. Many of the arts have a very long history, some connected with religion, like *Shao lin* boxing exercises which were supposed to have been developed to help the

A "honey-cart". Notice the wet-weather clothes and oil-cloth umbrellas.

Tai ji quan.

monks stay awake during long meditation sessions. *Tai ji quan*, popular in China with people of all ages, is a stylized form of fighting (performed without an opponent) which has been slowed down so that it is now a question of balance and muscular control rather than of speed and combat.

While specialists and those with great skill will practise their martial arts after work every day and may form teams to give demonstrations in China and abroad, most people who practise martial arts or any form of exercise, do so in the early morning, before work. If you go to any parks or open spaces before breakfast (between 5.30 and 7 am), you will find crowds of people, some doing *tai ji quan* together, others practising sword fighting, some doing faster forms of shadow-boxing, old people doing a five-minute series of exercises and, mixed in with these sports people, musicians practising in the open air, opera-singers trilling, trombonists and trumpeters playing against park walls and violinists doing their scales.

August

"Beginning of autumn; stopping of heat"

Army Day

Army Day on 1 August has a national significance, for the army plays an important role in Chinese society. The "People's Liberation Army" grew out of the Red Army which was formed in the late 1920s. The date chosen for Army Day commemorates the Nanchang uprising (1 August 1927), an unsuccessful attempt by the Communist forces to overthrow the local warlord, which also marked the beginning of the Communist Party's independent organization of its army after the break with the Guomindang (led by Chiang Kaishek). The newly formed army retreated into the mountains of Jiangxi province and was finally driven out by Chiang's troops. This second retreat was turned into a victory, as the army set off on the Long March to the northwest and there established the base from which both the war against Japan and the civil war against the Guomindang were directed.

The Red Army was used, not just as a fighting force, but as a social force, leading peasants to overthrow landlords, seize land and cultivate it for themselves at last. The Red Army organized mass campaigns in public health, in education and in public works, such as the irrigation of barren areas or the building of bridges, housing and roads.

The basis for army discipline, the "Three rules of discipline and the Eight points for attention", were very strictly enforced and were one of the reasons for the army's success. In traditional China, there had been a popular saying: "Don't make good iron into nails, don't make your sons into soldiers". It expressed the popular view that armies consisted of people who were little better than bandits. The Red Army helped to overcome the view of soldiers as murderers, rapists and thieves, by behaving exceptionally well, and helping peasants to improve their lives rather than running off with their chickens

THE LONG MARCH

After the break with the Guomindang in 1927, the Chinese Communists left the cities and set up "revolutionary base areas" in mountainous parts of China. One was in Jiangxi province in the Jinggang mountains. Chiang Kaishek (1887-1975) directed five encirclement campaigns at this base and finally, using a million men, he drove the Red Army out of Jiangxi. In October 1934 about 100,000 men and women of the Red Army began a march of 6,000 miles (9600 km) to another base area in the northwest, at Yan'an. Harassed most of the way by Chiang's troops, by warlords and by hostile tribesmen in remote mountain areas, they marched on foot through snowy mountains near the Tibetan borders, where many died or lost limbs through frost-bite. They marched through swampy grasslands, full of leeches and mosquitoes carrying black malaria, where, if soldiers or horses strayed, they would sink and drown in stinking water. In the grasslands, the soldiers were reduced to eating pine cones and berries and rats, and, like Charlie Chaplin in the film *The Gold Rush*, they apparently boiled up leather boots and drank the soup.

Only about 5,000 of those who had left Jiangxi a year before actually reached Yan'an in 1935. Some of the sick and wounded were left behind on the way. Mao Zedong and his second wife had to leave their two children behind with peasants and they were never found again. Some of the soldiers were left behind to continue guerrilla warfare against Chiang Kaishek, but thousands of marchers died of wounds, starvation and disease. For those who survived, the Long March is still an incredible epic, an illustration of the determination of the Communist armies to survive and continue the fight.

and their daughters.

This role of the army as educator and helper has continued. Students at school and university are encouraged to "learn from the army", not simply military techniques but also the idea of service. In every major building project in China you can still see hundreds of soldiers, running up and down with wheelbarrows, helping to build dams and roads and canals. It was in the army, too, that some of the techniques of Chinese traditional medicine were researched and developed. Army doctors discovered, for example, that many medicinal herbs used in the past have practical application today and, by experimenting on themselves, army doctors developed the use of acupuncture as a painkiller in operations.

Acupuncture

Acupuncture is a treatment used in China for centuries and consists of inserting very fine needles into the body to relieve pain. During the Cultural Revolution (1966-69) army doctors took up Mao Zedong's instruction to examine traditional medicine, which he said was a "treasure house". They followed another of his directives, "Make the past serve the present", and discovered that the traditional technique could successfully be used instead of western anaesthesia in surgical operations. This discovery was of importance in China which, as a poor country, has not yet got enough trained doctors or sufficient drugs and equipment for widespread medical treatment. Someone who has been trained in traditional acupuncture techniques needs only a few weeks of extra training and a handful of needles to be able to serve as an "anaesthetist" in operations. Acupuncture analgesia does not have bad side-effects or after-effects and is extremely cheap to use. It cannot be used on all patients or in all operations and research still goes on into how it works, but it has made a great difference to routine medical work in China.

Chinese soldiers. The army is composed of volunteers, who join for a couple of years, and some professional officers. The prestige of the army is high, though a soldier's equipment and uniform are basic.

Acupuncture treatment for short sight.

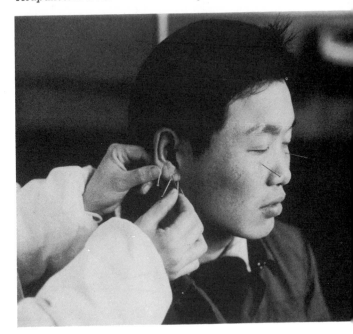

The Herd-Boy and the Spinning Girl

One of the most popular folk-tales of China, that of the herd-boy and the spinning girl, is remembered in mid-August. When flocks of magpies gather together, they are making a bridge across the Milky Way to unite the two lovers (represented by the constellations of Aquila and Lyra) who are separated by the "Heavenly River". The herd-boy was a poor orphan whose only friend was his old water buffalo. One day he was by the river, where the water buffalo wallowed in the mud, when he saw a group of beautiful girls bathing. He fell in love with one of them

47

The southwest of China is a rich and fertile rice-growing area. Peasants work against a scene of feathery bamboo and mountains which has inspired many painters.

and they married. Unfortunately, she was not a mortal but one of the spinning girls of the King of Heaven, who eventually snatched her back to heaven. Since then, the two lovers have only been allowed to meet once a year by crossing the magpie bridge. In the past, on 16 August, to celebrate the festival of the herd-boy and the spinning girl, girls used to test their skill at embroidery by floating a needle on a

◁ *Girls talk together as they plant out rice seedlings, near Guangzhou.*

POEM
written in the first century AD about the herd-boy and the spinning girl. The "Heavenly River" is the Milky Way.

Far, far the Herd-boy star,
Bright, bright the Spinning girl shines,
Slender, slender her white fingers move,
Click, click, the shuttle of her loom.
At dusk she has not finished her work,
Her tears fall like streaming rain.
The Heavenly River is clear and shallow,
They are separated by so little
Yet they cannot cross the river.
They gaze at each other but can never speak.

49

bowl of water. If the shadow cast by the needle was fine and clear (like a thread) or diffused (like flowers), they would be skilful, but if the needle cast a thick, stick-like shadow, they would be clumsy.

Harvest

Many children, office workers and students are taken out into the countryside in August to help with the wheat and rice harvests. China is still very under-mechanized, and so practically all agricultural work of planting, thinning, transplanting and harvesting is done by hand.

The wheat harvest comes first and must be quickly cleared so that a second grain sowing can be done immediately. In the hot, sub-tropical south, two or three grain crops are possible in a year, but in the north, near Beijing, there is a wheat crop first and then a rice harvest. Wheat is made into flour (the basis of noodles and dumplings and steamed breads which are eaten in north China instead of rice), but rice is the national staple. It used to be thought impossibly difficult to grow rice in the north, but recently more and more rice has been grown in north China. Rice is not only enjoyed at home, but is also an important export for the Chinese. Rice sold to Southeast Asia fetches a higher price than the Chinese pay (to the Canadians and others) for wheat to replace the exported rice.

Wheat is planted in narrow rows, between tall rows of maize, and must be cut with a little sickle. You have to be careful not to swipe at your legs and not to cut the unripe maize. Harvesting wheat is back-breaking work and some people go out in the early hours of the morning to do their six hours work before the sun gets up to add to the exhaustion. After the grain is husked, it is spread out on the road to dry.

September

"Autumn equinox; cold dew"

School

In September school begins again after the summer holidays. There are only two long holidays from school in China, at the Spring Festival or lunar New Year and in the summer. Children are quite likely to go to nursery schools if they live in cities and their mothers go out to work, but many children, in both city and countryside, are looked after by their grandparents at home until they go to primary school at the age of seven. Primary school lasts five years, after which most children go on to a junior middle school for three years. Further schooling depends on their ability as well as on the availability of upper middle schools (which are rare in the remote rural areas).

The school day is longer than ours, starting at 8 am or earlier and not ending till 4 or 5 pm, depending on whether the pupil continues with after-school activities. The school week, like the working week, is six days long.

The curriculum in a Chinese school is quite familiar. In primary schools the fundamental task is learning to read and

Children during the Cultural Revolution "combined education with productive labour". These children helped to build an extension to their school. . .

. . . and these girls made rheostats in a school factory.

write a language that is infinitely more complex in construction than English, as well as learning maths and some geography, history, hygiene and politics. In a secondary school, the following subjects are offered: Chinese language, politics, maths, English (the most popular foreign language), another foreign language (Japanese is currently second to English), physics, chemistry, art, singing, agriculture, physiology and hygiene, history, geography and gym and sports.

The Education System

The two factors which have had most effect on the Chinese education system are

THE CULTURAL REVOLUTION

The Cultural Revolution started in 1966 with an attack on a play written by the vice-mayor of Beijing, Wu Han. Apart from this beginning, it was an attack on all that Marxists call the superstructure, which is that part of the state not connected with the economy (the economic base) and covering culture and ideas and education and administration. Some people within the Communist Party felt that by the 1960s, though the economy was "socialist", the same could not be said of the cultural superstructure. Mao felt that the Party itself was becoming corrupt and said in 1964: "At present, you can buy a [Party] branch secretary for a few packets of cigarettes . . .".

The people most associated with the Cultural Revolution are Jiang Qing (Mao's third wife), Yao Wenyuan (in charge of the national newspaper, the *People's Daily*), Zhang Chunqiao (a writer on Communist theory) and Wang Hongwen, a worker from Shanghai who rose very quickly to power through the Cultural Revolution, which gave him the opportunity to criticize those in authority in his factory and then in the city of Shanghai itself. They are now referred to as "The Gang of Four". They attacked almost everyone in power, calling them "rightists" or "capitalist-roaders", and encouraged everyone in China to do the same within their factory, school, hospital or village. Eminent scientists were criticized for "separating themselves from the masses"; factory administrators were criticized for ignoring

"Revolutionary" art. Such huge posters, celebrating the unity of workers throughout the world, can be seen along many city streets, though they are gradually being replaced by advertisements for Chinese and western consumer goods.

their workers; headmasters were criticized for not teaching enough politics in school; and all these eminent and often elderly people found themselves working as cleaners in their institutes or sent away to the countryside for several years to toil in fields and think over their "mistakes".

The Cultural Revolution affected everyone in China, but science and the arts perhaps suffered most. Pure scientists were no longer able to carry out much research, and writers, actors, painters and dancers were restricted to a range of "revolutionary" art forms, dictated from above. They were persecuted if they did not obey.

In 1969 the Cultural Revolution was declared to be "over", but its effects were felt until 1976 when Mao Zedong died and the "Gang of Four", who had continued to enforce policies that grew out of the Cultural Revolution, was overthrown. In 1976 a reversal of the Cultural Revolution began, which in most ways meant a return to the 1950s and 1960s, with factory managers, research scientists, hospital administrators, painters, writers and performers reinstated. At the moment, very little remains of the Cultural Revolution, but in the future some of its effects may be re-examined.

poverty and politics. The fact that China is still a poor country means that there are still villages where there is no primary school. Even if there is a primary school, there may be no higher education, so that parents who wish their children to go on studying must arrange for them to travel every day to the next village or perhaps board in the nearest town. Since education is not entirely free (though it only costs about 75 pence per year in fees), there is a small disincentive to parents to keep up the struggle to continue the education of their children, especially where the children could otherwise be contributing to the family income by working in the fields. Nevertheless, education is highly regarded in China and the demand for school places exceeds the number available. It is also true that, particularly since 1949, great efforts and achieve-

ments have been made in increasing the availability of education, especially in the countryside.

The effect of politics on education has been varied. In the first years of the People's Republic, education was modelled on the system in the Soviet Union, but in the middle of the 1960s the system was turned upside down by the Cultural Revolution. In the Cultural Revolution exams were abolished because they were said to be "surprise attacks" on pupils by their teachers. Mao Zedong even said that people should cheat if they had exams because it was silly for someone to worry about a sum if the person next to him knew the answer. The curriculum was filled with politics, taught both directly and indirectly under the slogan "put politics in command". "Politics in command" in sciences, for example, meant that classes were taught by workers from chemical factories or working electricians, rather than learning from books or from pure scientists.

Politics meant learning about work from workers, and about agriculture and the hard life of a peasant from a peasant. Therefore, for example, university students spent at least half of their time outside the university, away from libraries and books and teachers, working in factories or fields. Children in school would also "combine education with productive labour" by working in small workshops in the school, perhaps doing finishing work for a local factory or, like one middle school in Beijing, making Chinese chess sets with wooden pieces that were sold throughout the city.

The aim of all this productive labour and the retreat from books was to reduce the distinction between mental and manual work, to prevent students from feeling superior to peasants because of their education, and to prevent them from assuming that they would get easy, well-paid jobs on graduation.

One of the effects of the Cultural Revolution on education was that it produced a great number of "worker-peasant-soldier" students but very few experts, and the need for at least some experts was increasingly felt. After the end of the Cultural Revolution and the "downfall of the Gang of Four", educational policy was, once again, reversed. Exams were re-introduced in 1977 and the new stress was on the urgent need, not for politics, but for well-trained scientists and specialists who would help China modernize and grow strong in competition with other nations. All schooling from kindergarten onwards became directed towards exams as a measure of academic achievement and, consequently, social advancement. The passion to succeed academically has become so intense that recent issues of the magazine for young people, *Zhongguo qingnian*, have contained many articles explaining that failure in exams is not a disgrace and that the country needs street sweepers and workers as well as intellectuals.

During the Cultural Revolution, the most stress had been laid on giving extra encouragement to students from rural areas who did not have academic backgrounds, and such students often gained university places, not on the grounds of academic merit but because they were good members of their commune or effective Party members. As "worker-peasant-soldier" students filled the universities, academic standards were forced to drop. With the new stress on academic standards rather than political merit, students from rural areas were at a disadvantage since their schools and teachers could not cope with the demands. But in the national university entrance exams, the pass-mark for peasant competitors has been set lower than that for students from better-equipped and better-staffed city schools.

The Moon Festival

The most important traditional festival in September is the Moon Festival (at the full moon). People used to go up onto hills and mountains to admire the moon, carrying paper lanterns shaped like fish and birds. They would make a sacrifice by burning moon papers, which bore three pictures: at the top a picture of a Boddhisattva sitting cross-legged against the full moon; underneath that, a picture of a cassia tree; and below that, a rabbit pounding an elixir of immortality in a mortar. The rabbit and toad are still considered to be animals that live on the moon, though in China today, if people climb hills to watch the full moon rising, it is more for fun than to make sacrifices.

In Hong Kong and Taiwan, it is still customary to offer moon cakes to friends and business associates at the Moon Festival. These are rather heavy round cakes made of pastry with many different stuffings, from red bean paste to almond paste and eggs. They are made in moulds and glazed and the top is patterned with characters meaning "good luck" and other lucky things.

Chinese shadow puppets depicting the moon-hare.
The Chinese believed that a hare lived on the moon
and mixed an elixir of immortality for the gods.
A three-legged toad is also supposed to live on the
moon which he occasionally swallows, causing an
eclipse.

October

"Cold dew; frost's descent"

In October, persimmons ripen on the trees, bright orange against a blue sky. They are round, soft fruits which look rather like tomatoes but are very sweet. They can be eaten fresh or are often dried by being laid out on the roofs of houses in the autumn sun until they are brown and chewy.

National Day

National Day in China is 1 October. On Taiwan it is 10 October and called the "Double tenth" because it falls on the tenth day of the tenth month. In Hong Kong,

---

THE CIVIL WAR 1927-1949

The civil war in China was fought between the Guomindang and the Communist Party. When Sun Yatsen was leader of the Guomindang (1912-25), the two parties had been allied against the warlords. But when Chiang Kaishek succeeded Sun as the head of the Guomindang, he turned upon his allies and, from 1927 onwards, directed most of his military energy to suppressing Communists.

The civil war was complicated (and some might say decisively affected) by the full-scale Japanese invasion of China in 1937. The Japanese had been increasing their economic hold on China throughout the 1920s and finally invaded, with disastrous effect on the peasant population which was already suffering from terrible famines that were killing millions and tens of millions. The Japanese were very brutal in the invasion of north China, carrying out a "three alls" policy, which meant "burn all, kill all, destroy all", and leaving villages and agricultural land, roads and bridges quite ruined behind them.

Chiang Kaishek was pledged to resist the Japanese invasion and, when Pearl Harbour brought the allies into war with Japan, received very substantial military and economic aid to do so. As the war dragged on, even American advisors and generals began to doubt the seriousness of Chiang's anti-Japanese war and compared it unfavourably with the valiant battles fought by the Chinese Communists. In Yan'an, the Communists were blockaded by Chiang's troops so that no supplies of weapons, food or even medicine could get through (unless smuggled) but, with home-made weapons, soldiers growing their own food, and doctors experimenting with make-shift bandages and drugs, the Communists led the peasants against the Japanese.

The strength of Communist resistance, compared with Chiang Kaishek's nationalist army which was badly led, badly paid and consequently inclined to desert, had a great effect on the patriotic Chinese who increasingly rallied to the Communist cause. This appeal to patriotism, combined with steady work to improve the livelihood of the peasants, went a long way to guaranteeing the eventual victory of the Communist Party in the civil war.

where some people support the People's Republic and some support the Nationalists on Taiwan, you can see the red flag with its yellow stars flying on 1 October, soon followed by the Taiwanese flag, which is red and blue with a white sun pattern.

1 October is the day on which Mao Zedong proclaimed the founding of the People's Republic of China in 1949. This marked the end of a civil war which had raged since 1927. Civil wars are always painful since they divide the country and even divide family loyalties, and there is never a very satisfactory solution. In China the Nationalist forces led by Chiang Kaishek were driven out to the island of Taiwan where Chiang ruled over the "Republic of China" until his death in 1975. Both Chinas recognize that Taiwan is part of China and both claim to be the legitimate government of the whole country, but Chiang was at a disadvantage since he controlled only 9 million people (against the 1,000 million in the mainland).

National Day is celebrated in much the same way as May Day with all the parks open and full of flowers, fairground stalls and public performances of songs, dances and plays. Everyone has a day off to celebrate and occasionally there are vast parades of sportsmen and women, children waving paper flowers and dancers in bright costumes in the great central Square of Heavenly Peace in Beijing.

November

"Slight snow; great snow"

Winter Clothes

November marks the beginning of winter. In the past, those officials who had permission from the Emperor to wear sable fur coats used to put them on on the first day of November, though they kept the fur turned out. Today, in the depths of winter, some Chinese still wear fur coats, but with the fur lining on the inside, where it is warmer. It also used to be considered necessary to send winter clothing to the ancestors. Funeral shops sold paper cut-out clothes and these would be burnt at the gate of the house, so that they joined the ancestral spirits in the spirit world.

Nowadays, not everyone wears a fur coat in winter. Instead, people wear several layers of clothes under thick padded cotton coats. The outer coats are made of a thick layer of cotton wadding, sandwiched between an inner and outer layer of cotton cloth. Those who can afford it might use silk wadding, for this is very insulating and much lighter than cotton wadding.

Both men and women wear trousers in winter and these, too, are padded. Since very little rain (or even snow) falls in winter in China, winter shoes are also made of padded cotton, with thick soles made of many layers of cotton cloth. Underneath their padded outer clothes, people wear up to six layers — many of them cotton tee-shirts and track-suit trousers in brilliant colours which show at the ankle. Over the top of the cotton

SHANGHAI

Shanghai is the largest city in China with a population of over 12 million (in 1975), living in the highest population density in China. Until the middle of the nineteenth century and the forced opening of China to the west, Shanghai was not a very important place. Then the Europeans established a trading centre and built lots of banks, vast stone office blocks and fine residences. For a while the foreign residents ran the "international concession" in Shanghai with their own police and their own jurisdiction, but when the Japanese invaded in 1937 most of them left, and after 1949 the city became completely Chinese again in all but architecture. As you walk through the streets, you can still see French château-style houses, Scottish baronial castles, Methodist churches and mock Tudor houses, all turned to different uses now but still distinctively European. On some of the walls there are still very faded advertisements for Parker Pens, and some of the post-boxes are English, with Queen Victoria's crest on them, though they have now been painted green (which is the colour of Chinese post-boxes).

Shanghai has a special significance in China, for it is regarded as the most fashionable city, a place of greater excitement than normal, and the source of all sorts of new ideas. If you walk along the Nanjing Road,

Shopping for winter clothes in the First Department Store, the largest in Shanghai.

Acrobats' circus in Shanghai.

the main shopping centre, you can see straight away that people's clothes are smarter, women and men both have more daring hair-styles, and the atmosphere is that of a great city, whereas Beijing, for example, feels more like a sleepy country town.

That Shanghai is China's most densely populated city is obvious. On a Sunday (which is a day off for most people) the Nanjing Road is so crowded that Christmas shopping in London's Oxford Street would seem in comparison, like solitary confinement.

Another legacy of the imperialist past in Shanghai is the number of restaurants and shops serving western food. There are cake shops where you can buy cream horns, *pingguo pai* (apple pie), *qiaokeli pai* (chocolate tart) or *lingmeng pai* (lemon meringue pie) and restaurants where you can eat hamburgers and drink coffee.

Shanghai in summer . . .

. . . and Shanghai in winter. The people's outline changes and they look much broader as they put on their padded clothes against the cold. In winter, instead of saying "How are you?", people ask "How many layers are you wearing?"

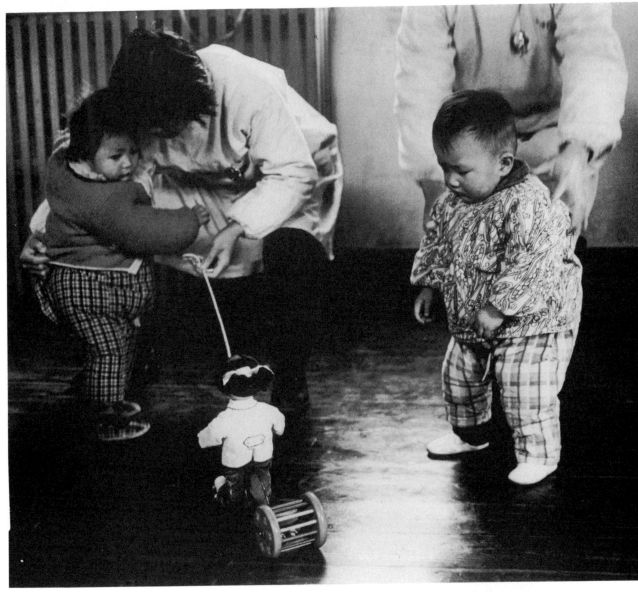

Brightly clothed children in the nursery of a machine tool plant, Shanghai.

padded jackets, girls wear brightly flowered cotton jackets (which can be washed more easily than the padded jackets) and men wear light grey jackets with high collars and little frogged buttons.

In the past, peasant clothes tended to be blue or black and today's working clothes are still mostly blue. Old people, too, stick to dark colours. In winter, old ladies look very impressive in black velvet jackets with black satin padded trousers tied tightly at the ankle over their white socks, and tiny bound feet in black velvet slippers.

Young people wear bright underwear and jumpers with rainbow stripes under their cotton jackets, and girls have blouses in all sorts of bright colours with embroidered collars. But the most colourful dressers in China are children and babies. Their clothes

The Great Wall.

THE GREAT WALL

Some 70 kilometres northwest of Beijing is the fort of Badaling, on the Great Wall. A train full of tourists leaves Beijing Station every morning at 9.30 to arrive at Badaling about an hour later. It is possible to reach Badaling by bus, but you would have to change at least once on the way from the city centre and the trip, though cheaper than the train, would take a couple of hours.

At Badaling you can climb the steep wall that rises up over the hills and look out to the land beyond which stretches to Mongolia. The wall snakes endlessly over the mountains, for it is some 4000 kilometres long, so extensive that it is the only man-made building recognizable from the moon.

Even as early as the fifth century BC rival states in north China constructed walls to protect themselves. In 221 BC, when the Qin Emperor defeated all the other states to unite China, he linked up some of the existing walls to protect China from external threat. During succeeding centuries, the Wall was lengthened and strengthened, the last great building and repair programme being carried out during the Ming dynasty (1368-1644). The Ming was perhaps most nervous about threats from the Mongols and Manchus (to the northwest and northeast), for the previous dynasty had been a Mongol one and, in 1644, the Manchus were to sweep through the Wall, defeat the Ming and establish the Qing dynasty.

The Wall is high (6.6-7.8 metres) and wide enough for several horses to gallop abreast along the top. Dotted along it are small forts and watchtowers where the garrisons used to live.

Now it is a tourist centre, for both Chinese and foreigners. The first visitors arrive soon after dawn, sending Siberian chipmunks, laughing jays and hares back into the trees and hills, to re-appear when the last visitors leave at dusk. At Badaling there are small snack bars where you can buy tea, bread, biscuits and fruit to fortify you for the steep climb up to the forts.

are miniature versions of their parents', but in red or blue floral patterned material. Babies and small children in China do not wear nappies but have "split pants" until they are about three. This means that they can squat wherever they like and their parents and grandparents have to keep a watchful eye in order to keep the house and street clean. In winter, split pants could give babies very cold bottoms and so over their padded jackets and padded split pants, they wear a sort of padded apron, back and front, and look like little Emperors in their brilliant clothes.

Vegetables

The ground freezes over so that nothing can be grown in north China until the thaw in March. The problem of getting fresh vegetables is solved by the last crop in late October — the cabbage harvest. This is the Chinese cabbage, known in England by its Cantonese name, *Bok choy*, or as "Chinese leaves". It is sold when in glut so that people buy enormous quantities to last them through the winter. If it is kept on a north-facing balcony or in a pit dug in the cold ground, it will last till spring, though people are rather fed up with it by then!

Among the other rare fresh vegetables available are tomatoes and cucumbers, grown in winter greenhouses. These are not permanent glass structures, but are built out of earth every November and ploughed flat in spring. An earth wall is built, bamboo stakes are stuck into it and bent down to the earth to form a frame and this is covered with polythene sheets. At night, straw matting is rolled over the polythene to protect the vegetables from frosts. These greenhouses work very well for there is sun throughout the Chinese winter although the nights are ferociously cold.

The same method is used for building the earth walls of greenhouses as was used for building the city walls and even the Great Wall. A wooden framework (two parallel

sets of planks, held in place by a cross-beam) is set on the ground and earth is shovelled into it. Every fifteen centimetres or so the earth is pounded flat with wooden tamps and another layer is piled on top. Up to twenty layers will make a wall about a metre high which will stand well when the frame is moved on to build the next section. Because the earth and atmosphere are fairly dry, the wall is quite stable (and archaeologists have found walls built in this way that are thousands of years old). In spring, the greenhouse walls are ploughed flat to make way for the spring planting.

There is a simple explanation for the lengths that northern Chinese go to to provide vegetables for themselves during the

A vegetable stall. There is not much variety of fresh vegetables available in winter.

long cold winter. Though south China can produce fruit and vegetables throughout its milder winter, there are not enough trucks, lorries, trains, roads or boats to transport food from one area to the next on a great scale. There is also a political explanation: regional self-sufficiency is considered a good method of defence against war and also gives people practice in overcoming difficulties themselves rather than relying on others to bale them out.

December

Beating the Cold

December is fiercely cold in much of China, with temperatures of −8°C to −20°C in the north, while in the south, though it does not drop much below freezing, people can feel almost as cold, since there is little heating in houses or offices. Outdoors, and even indoors, people wear their thick padded clothes, and in the north, they spend as

Clearing the streets of snow. Two women carry a basket of snow to the pile at the side of the road.

MAO ZEDONG (1893-1976)

Mao was born in 1893 into a reasonably well-off peasant family. His father did not want his son to spend too much time at school, though he allowed him to get enough education to be able to keep the family accounts. Mao was obviously strong-willed, even as a child, for he fought to be allowed to continue his education and also refused a child-bride whom his father chose for him when he was about twelve. He was never to forget certain scenes of his childhood — starving peasants attacking landlords' houses, their brutal execution, their heads hanging outside the city gates till they rotted away.

He went to Beijing where he worked in the University Library and attended seminars on Marxism. He married Yang Kaihui, daughter of one of the progressive professors at the University, and was a founding member of the Chinese Communist Party which first met in 1921. Throughout the early years of the Communist Party, Mao stuck firmly to his belief in the revolutionary potential of the peasants, against the line that was recommended by the Soviet Union, that only workers could lead a socialist revolution (since that was what Marx had written and what had happened in Russia). The question led to disagreements and splits within the Party, which was finally forced by circumstances to rely on the peasants, who did, as Mao had predicted, reveal themselves as determined revolutionaries, ready to fight for their right to hold land and improve their living conditions.

Mao's own life was much affected by the events that led to the Communist Party's move to the countryside. In 1927 Chiang Kaishek broke the official alliance between the Guomindang and Communist Party by massacring thousands of workers in Shanghai. After this first defeat, the Communists were no longer safe in the cities which were dominated by the Guomindang. Among the Communists caught in the cities was Mao's wife, Yang Kaihui, mother of his two young sons, who was executed in 1930. Losses like these forced the Communist Party into the countryside and to adopt guerrilla war tactics which Mao and his associates directed with great skill.

During the Long March (see page 46), at the Zunyi Conference in 1934, Mao became Chairman of the Communist Party of China. Later, when the Communists were based at Yan'an, he devoted more of his time to writing articles than to the administration of the Party. The articles that he wrote, on politics and culture, formed the basis for his future government.

On 1 October 1949 the civil war was won and Mao announced the founding of the People's Republic of China. As well as being Chairman of the Communist Party, he became Chairman of the People's Republic, a position he held until 1959 when he resigned to devote himself to writing and research once again. During the early years of the People's Republic, Mao continued to stress the role of the peasants as he had done since the 1920s, but this view now brought him into increasing conflict with the Soviet Union. In 1958 he launched the "People's Communes", large agricultural units, bigger than an English county, where central facilities were provided, partly by the state, and all agricultural land was worked by communal effort. This "socialization" of agriculture did not please the Soviet Union which believed that industry should be developed before agriculture was re-organized. Mao believed that better results would be achieved by increasingly collective work and by exploiting the different conditions of the larger unit.

In 1959 Mao was succeeded as Chairman of the People's Republic by Liu Shaoqi who was later to suffer during the Cultural

Chairman Mao's portrait hangs over the entrance to the Forbidden City in Beijing. In 1949 he proclaimed the founding of the People's Republic standing on this gate which has become the national symbol of China. On either side of his portrait are slogans: "Long live the People's Republic of China" and "Long live the unity of the peoples of the world".

Revolution. Mao retained his position as Party Chairman and spent much time travelling the country, looking at the results of his plans and policies. There is no question that his influence was still enormous and that, when he felt the Party was corrupt, he could launch a movement like the Cultural Revolution even though he had no governmental or military position.

During and after the Cultural Revolution, it became apparent that Mao's health was failing and he appeared less often in public. The last years of his life were marked by the great unpopularity of his last wife, Jiang Qing, and her closeness to Mao detracted from his own popularity. Nevertheless, his achievements before the "Liberation" of 1949, his ability to see where China's strength lay at a time when the whole country seemed exhausted, will not be forgotten.

Sitting on the kang.

much time as possible in their houses which are heated by little stoves burning day and night. The stoves burn coal balls, mixed from coal-dust and mud. The coal-dust is cheap to buy and it is mixed with mud into a black paste and spread out on the pavement to dry. When it is the consistency of fudge, it is cut up into squares which are rolled about in a basket until the lumps are roughly circular, and ready to use in little stoves or in cooking.

A feature of houses in north China is the *kang* or brick bed. A brick platform is built against the south wall of the house and since it is hollow, a stove can be placed underneath. Sometimes the flue from the stove is led under the *kang* and then outside, and this

Sitting on the kang.

makes an extra source of under-bed heating. Straw mats are laid on the brick surface and then underquilts and overquilts, so that it is quite comfortable to sleep on. In winter, people spend much more of their time sitting on the *kang*, sewing, studying or doing household tasks, warmed from underneath.

Winter Food

Winter brings special foods like *tang hulu* or toffee-apples, which are not as we know them but a whole row of little red crabapples speared on a stick and covered in toffee. These are sold along the streets and in parks like the Summer Palace and at the Temple of Heaven. In restaurants, a favourite winter meal is Mongolian hot-pot. This is cooked at the table, either in individual stoves fuelled with charcoal or, at special communal tables, on a charcoal stove standing in the middle under a great basin filled with boiling water. Everyone is served with plates of mutton sliced paper-thin, sliced spring onions, Chinese cabbage, rice noodles and tiny dumplings. Each person dips a piece of mutton into the boiling water, holding it with his wooden chopsticks for a minute until it is cooked, then dips it into the many sauces that accompany the meal. The vegetables, rice noodles and dumplings are all tipped into the water to boil while the meat is eaten, and provide a delicious soup by the end of the meal.

Another Mongolian winter meal is a kind of hamburger. This, too, is cooked on a special table. In this case the table is heated from underneath by a charcoal stove, but the top is a smooth, flat metal surface and this is used for cooking. Guests are given bowls of finely minced mutton, egg, spring onions and sauces which they mix into a burger shape and cook themselves. The burgers are put into sesame buns and eaten. Both these Mongolian meals are very warming, especially as you stand or sit around a heated table.

Drink

In summer, Chinese men drink quite a lot of beer, either bottled beer from Qingdao (which was a German colony, and the beer industry was started there by the Germans) or locally made beer, which is usually flat, since it is kept in basins and kettles and served by the jug. Like the Qingdao beer, it resembles lager. In winter, however, men drink warmed wines, like the Japanese rice wine called *sake*.

The Chinese wines are also made from grain, some from rice, although the most famous, Shaoxing wine, is made from millet. Such wines have been drunk hot in China since the beginning of the Bronze Age (c.1700 BC), when many of the fine bronze vessels used in rituals and placed in royal tombs were intended for the heating, serving and drinking of warm wine.

Mao Zedong

26 December was the birthday of Mao Zedong. It has never been a national holiday but is marked in red in the calendar and sometimes there are special editorials in the newspapers commemorating him.

Books for Further Reading

Anthology of Chinese Literature edited by Cyril Birch, Penguin Books (1965)

The Chinese by David Bonavia, Allen Lane (1981)

An economic geography of China by Thomas R. Tregear, Butterworth (1970)

Mao for Beginners by Rius and Friends, Writers and Readers Publishing Coop (1980)

A Year in Upper Felicity: life in a Chinese village during the Cultural Revolution by Jack Chen, Harrap (1973)

Index

915.1
W

14623

Through the year in China

DATE DUE			
OCT 23 '68			
Nov 11, 84			
NOV 3 1991			
2/19/98